HEART BEAT

My Life
with Jack & Neal

by
Carolyn Cassady

Creative Arts Book Company
Berkeley • 1976

Letters of Allen Ginsberg, Jack Kerouac, Neal Cassady
and Carolyn Cassady appear through the courtesy of
the University of Texas.

Heart Beat is an excerpt from a work-in-progress
tentatively entitled *The Third Word*.

Published by Creative Arts Book Company,
833 Bancroft Way, Berkeley, CA 94710.

Distributed by Book People,
2940 Seventh Street, Berkeley, CA 94710.

ISBN 0-916870-03-0 (paper)
ISBN 0-916870-04-0 (signed limited cloth)
Library of Congress Card Catalog #76-12732

This little book is dedicated to Barry Gifford,
whose idea was the father and his patience
the mother.

C.C.

Contents

PART ONE

Spring 1952

Chapter One

Dear Jack:

Alright now listen you, let's get serious. You going to write another book, huh? I'm trying to write one, right? You love me, don't you? I love you, don't I? If we're so all-fired good, then think of the funny times historians of future will have in digging up period in last half of 51 when K lived with C, much like Gauguin and Van Gogh, or Neitche and Wagner, or anybody and how, during this time of hard work and reorientation C learned while K perfected his art and how under the tutoring of the young master K, C ironed out much of his word difficulties and in the magnificent attic K did his best work and etc. etc. etc. No, but listen now, you'd have perfect freedom, great place in which to write, car to cut around in, satisfaction of knowing you're helping me when I need it most. No bother, great books to read, music to hear, life to see, up at any hour, to bed at same, free rent, best of all, a ral period wherein instead of, when you're actually at a weak point as now, going thru hassel and money spending of setting up own pad... as you just got thru doing . . . you come to me for rest and relaxation and find a spot with absolutely everything you could need already set up for you.

All you have to do is take advantage of my hospitality, like a weekend that stretches into months in an English countryside estate, and say to yourself that you need a quiet place of freedom in which to write a new book and bone up on those few things you might hanker to know while you've got the chance to just lie around doing so, a time in which to gather your strength and your thoughts, a period of recuperation wherein you solidify your soul, everything is not jazz, cunt and kicks as you know so well, and before you indulge in same by taking off for some faraway place before you're really ready, you must come here to listen to me and make into cement the liquid putty of our life.

I have absolutely greatest bed in the world on the floor of my extraordinary attic; I got books and shelves, great huge desk that's bigger than any desk could possibly be, since Carolyn made it out of 6 ft. by 6 ft. piece of plywood, with immense dictionary of 30 lbs., and foot thick proportions, and fine lamps and good radio (one downstairs too) and wondrous taperecorder made for not only endless kicks on sound but for dictaphone type writing and recording of thoughts, hi and otherwise, and golf clubs, and baseballs and (soon) tennis racquets with nearby court and all the socks, handkerchiefs and dirty pictures one could want, and perfect weather, no heat, no cold, and world famous galleries and railroad you must dig, and Al Hinkle and maybe Bill Tomson and whore houses, if you've got the money, and freedom, man, freedom, no bull, Carolyn loves you, be like your mama without you having any need to cater like to her, and coffee, gobs of expensive coffee, and clothes washed free, and your portrait painted, and front parlor for smooching with anything handy (before you go upstairs for complete privacy) and good typewriter and ribbon, and the greatest of subtle think drugs, and so soft and easy to take: Dexedrine, it's perfect and mellow and is such a mental wonder that on it I write poetry (after a fashion) I got lots of it and journals and paper and if you don't come home for days or stay in your room for days or sleep forever or stay up all night or growl or cuss or dig my gone little chicks who are positively no bother even to a child-hater like Dillinger (much less than even Julie or master Bill, Jr.) or if you want to get serious again like an idealistic youth and want to really get in there on some subject, whether by yourself or with me, or if you want to go to pot so as to be further prepared for a tropical clime, or if you want analyst at free

4

clinic (50¢ a visit) or if you want to work on R.R. or any damn old thing that strikes your fancy, do all of it, it's OK, more than you can possibly realize, for you don't know what easy living is til you dig old man C's brand at 29 Russell.

As soon as you get tired of us you may, if you are prepared in your own mind, leave at once for your shangri-la, or else, if you succeed in finding a bit of peace, or in doing a work that can't be quickly abandoned, you will stay here until December, at which time we will all pile into my station wagon with its roominess and very slowly dig everything as we drive to Mex City where we will stay until short money completely fades and then the wife, little kiddies and I will bid you fond goodby and leave you to your own devices in that city of magic. All this with less tension and anxieties than one might experience with even Mr. Burroughs' family, for Carolyn and I, at last, are a smooth running little team, that tho we sputter and snort a bit, are compatible as hell.

Naturally, in the back of your mind must be the remembrance of the rough receptions you've received at 29 Russell in the past, in fact, less than 2 years ago, but you must concede it was not as difficult for you as a murder or suicide might have made such a brief visit. Carolyn wants to try and make it up to you. We could try by way of a few group orgies or whatever, although this might sensibly be postponed until after Oct. because she's as big as our house and the bed is only four feet across. You understand that if you don't come here now it will curse my new son forever, since you won't be here to be his Godfather, and because you will have deserted him, I would be forced to not name him John Allen Cassady as is my present intent.

And be sure and bring your Bongo drums, or you'll have to go down on O'Farrell and see the gone drums there.

Early AM

Just got back from daily passenger run . . . I'm a big passenger brakie now, with a pretty monkey-suit that looks like a tux from the rear . . . and can't think of much more to say that might entice you to cover the long trail to this end of the world for no good reason, except that it's too hot in NY or Mex and too European in France and too trite in Great Neck and too early for Siberia or Africa. Incidentally, when all is lost you and I will go to Morocco and build railroad for thousand a month. All we do is ride while African coolies dump ballast over roadbed.

Am dying to read *On the Road* so you better have it published quick or have spare ms. And if you don't come because of intellectual reasons or because you just feel you can't make it, I will understand just as I think I do about poor J, and if I pine and die away as she without you: just meant to be.

N.

The event Neal had anticipated and promoted throughout 1951 finally occurred: Jack arrived. We had thought and talked of it so much, the actualization was extremely awkward for awhile. Neal bounded about showing Jack in rapid succession the wonders he had described in his letters, overdoing it, clowning and reducing Jack to giggles as he followed Neal about. I was straining everything to be agreeable, as was Jack, but we remained shy and formal most of the time for many days.

Jack and J, his second wife, had broken completely and bitterly. "You see," he explained to me, "she was an only child; raised by women, her mother and aunts. They all hated men and they taught her to, too. They were dedicated to revenge and used me to vent their anger

. . . it's true; I'm convinced they did it on purpose.

"I caught her with this Puerto Rican a couple of times, see, and now she's pregnant and says it's my child . . . HA . . . it ain't *my* child."

He seemed sick at heart but certain, though I wondered how he could be so sure. J's betrayal hurt him deeply, especially since she was the second wife to reject him. I felt really sorry for him and found it hard to understand why his judgment in choosing wives was so poor. I had only heard him talk sympathetically about women in general and quite sentimentally about marriage and family life.

He was immediately at ease with children, sharing an understanding at their level and communicating naturally without being maudlin. I never got the impression that my girls were a nuisance to him; rather he sought their company, listened intently to Cathy's prattle and told her stories far richer and more alive than those I'd read to her. He was unaccustomed to small babies, however, and didn't know what to do with them. On hearing him say something to this effect, Neal scooped up John from his crib and thrust him at Jack.

"No, man, here . . . babies are to *hold,* see? Just feel that. You've never known . . . see? You gotta *hold* 'em."

Surprised and awkward, Jack still chuckled at this sudden outburst of Neal's and tried to do as he said. John reared his head back to study the strange new face a moment, then sunk relaxed against Jack's chest. Jack did his best, patted him hesitantly, but obviously felt he had a bag of eggs and was relieved to have me take him from him. Neal all the while was raving about the advantages of tiny babies over older children.

7

The first few weeks I didn't see much of Jack. He'd go with Neal, wander off on his own or stay in his room reading or writing. The attic worked well for him. He settled in and carefully arranged the few precious books and papers he needed to make him feel at home. As Neal had told him, I had found a huge piece of plywood and with the aid of orange crates (which also served to hold books) constructed a great desk, the surface smoothed with several coats of dark green enamel. It could hardly fail to inspire a writer, I felt.

Only half the attic was "finished," but Jack preferred it that way. The rough, bare other half lent a barn effect and satisfied his craving for the natural and simple. The end he occupied was far from complete or decorated either, but it was cozy and snug. A box spring and mattress made a low "pad" and was covered with a paisley spread. The one window and its dark green shade was softened somewhat by burlap curtains. One square striped rug covered the bare floor boards and added a touch of color and warmth. He was gratifyingly enthusiastic. The only uncomfortable aspect for Jack was that the only access to and from his lair was a door in Neal's and my bedroom... as was the only route to the bathroom. It surprised me to find him so shy, old-fashioned and modest about personal physical needs or habits, but he used the bathroom only when no one was around and made arrangements elsewhere whenever possible. We all tried to cater to his embarrassment, though it was somewhat difficult with small children, and I had to be careful to be fully clothed at all times.

He had arrived at the worst time for hiring out as a brakeman, but after a few weeks Neal managed to get him a job in the baggage room at the depot. This eased things a bit, as Jack was forever fearful of imposing on us; this way he felt more independent. Neal's work was slower now, and they were able to spend more time together.

Although they verbalized some awareness of my feelings, and the situation was all right on the surface, I was no less anxious or content. By now, though, I realized I had to find a means of dealing with this if I wanted to keep Neal and the family together; it seemed an inevitable condition. I mentally searched and probed for attitudes and answers that would fit some reasonable precedent in the institution of marriage. It wasn't that it was uncommon for extra or unrelated persons to live in a household . . . in fact such had often been the case in my own home; we were always taking in medical students or associates. But I knew this was different, though I tried my best to view it in a tolerant light. Each time they went gaily out the door or shut themselves up in the attic, I could not overcome the feeling of being a neglected household drudge.

It took a great deal of effort for me not to show how I felt and to search for reasonable criteria on which to base a change in my feelings, and a physical reaction soon erupted.

Chapter Two

It was Neal's birthday. He had worked the day before and slept late. Jack had left the house before either of us were up. Neal and I were having a pleasant homey day, exchanging comments on trivia as he drank coffee and I puttered about the chores. As the afternoon waned, I was aware of an increasing ache and numbness on the left side of my face. By dinner time it was growing quite alarming. Although I was trying to dismiss it, Neal's sympathy and our curiosity as to the cause finally persuaded me to call a doctor friend.

The doctor recognized the symptoms as Bell's palsy and was adamant that I should get to the clinic as soon as possible. Meanwhile he would send a prescription for pain.

"What causes it?" I couldn't think of anything I could have done to the left side of my face.

"No one knows for sure. Soldiers used to get it from long exposure to cold on one side, like an open train window."

"That certainly lets me out. How could I possibly get something like this?"

"Can't tell, though there is a suspicion it may result from emotional strain also." Now then, the good doctor was getting warmer. At any rate, he said it used to be incurable, but now physical therapy could usually do it if caught in time. Then I remembered a music teacher my sister had had. One whole side of her face was drawn up, the mouth crooked and inclined to drool, the eye wide and staring. I shuddered at the frightening prospect.

As often happened in emergencies, it was a Friday

night, so I could do nothing about it until Monday. Neal went out to the pharmacy for the prescription, and I put it out of my mind as best I could so we could enjoy his birthday dinner. I had splurged on steak and wine, and I wondered where Jack was. Had he forgotten it was Neal's birthday? Didn't seem likely. Perhaps he felt he'd be intruding, thinking we'd prefer to be alone. Whatever his reason, he didn't appear. We let the girls stay up for the package unwrapping and the small cake with the candles. Although Neal always made much over any gift, they were just the usual necessities like socks, handkerchiefs and underwear.

After the children had been read to and tucked in, Neal and I relaxed with another glass of wine and a cigarette. He was concerned about my face and pain, and I felt close to him, relaxed and content. When we went to bed he was tender and "with me," reviving my hopes for our sex life. A lovely day, I mused as I drifted into sleep. All would be well.

The shrill ring of the phone jolted Neal out of bed to quell it before it woke the children. I was more slowly aroused, partially from the codeine. Hearing Neal's anxious tone, I struggled to listen more attentively.

"Yeah . . . of course . . . you're *where?* My God, man, whaja do? Never mind, I'll be right down . . . right," and he rushed back to the bedroom and began grabbing for clothes.

"Jack's in jail. Gotta go get him out." He hopped about getting his other foot through the jeans.

"In *jail?* Oh, no, Neal . . . what for?"

"Don't know yet. I'll go see. He sounded boiled though." He slapped the belt end through the loop and bent to make a few swift pats at his hair.

"Gosh, I hope it isn't serious. Just when everything was going so well. What could he have done? Poor Jack. But do hurry won't you? What time is it?"

"Just after twelve." He leaned over the bed to kiss me and ran out the door.

The rest of the night was one of growing restlessness, anxiety and pain. They didn't come back, and the codeine was wearing off. Before I realized it was too late for further sleep, the girls awoke and began padding about their room. John's squeaks and coos emanated from the other room, and the day had begun.

When their needs were all met, and Neal and Jack had still not appeared, I washed my hair and rolled it up. Just as I secured the last roller, I heard voices and action in the front hall. When I opened the bathroom door, I saw Neal darting down the kitchen stairs and Jack escorting a young black woman up his attic steps. Stunned, I followed Neal. Downstairs Neal was busy lighting the stove under the teakettle and rattling cups not looking up at me as I came down the stairs. I tried to keep my voice level. "What's going on, Neal? Where have you been? I see you got Jack out of jail, what was it?"

"Do we have any sugar?" He wasn't as calm as he tried to sound, I knew that, and he knew where the sugar was kept, so I didn't answer, just stood there by the stove confronting him. "Well, actually, you see ... ah ... you see Jack wasn't actually in jail ... " and he tried to laugh like it was nothing, waving a spoon around. "He was terribly drunk and he thought it would be a joke to get me out of the house that way ... he didn't really mean anything by it, honey. ..." He had bounded to the refrigerator and was

12

peering in as though it had no back to it.

The sickening wave of familiar feelings welling up in me made me clamp my mouth shut and go sit down by the table. I was shaking and trying not to fly apart; I couldn't speak. Finally I stood up and spat out in low icy tones: "You certainly don't think I'm going to put up with *that* sort of thing in my home? With the *children?*" and I flung my head and rolled my eyes upward like some Biblical evangelist. "You just get yourself right up there and get-her-out-of-my-house RIGHT NOW!" In another second I would scream or break something so I dashed for the stairs and ran to hide in the bathroom.

I'd forgotten how I looked. My face was there in the mirror with no makeup and the rollers, only it wasn't my face but the violin teacher's with the crooked mouth and unblinking eye. I covered it with my hands to shut out the sight. I could hear Neal knocking at the attic door calling up to Jack, but I couldn't hear the words. I was sitting on the edge of the tub, trembling, when I remembered the children. I grabbed a scarf and fumbled to tie it over the rollers as I rushed out the door. I knew I had to get to them first.

Too late. Just as I got to the end corner of our bed, Jack and the girl jumped down from the attic steps. Cathy and Jamie were standing in their doorway beyond, and Neal stood leaning against the bureau near the hallway door. I had to stop to let Jack and the girl pass. Instead the girl swished up to me sneering and let fly a stream of curses and abuse. I stood immobile in surprise. To stem the torrent I tried weakly to insert I had nothing against her personally, nor was it any concern of mine what Jack did, but this was my home, and I'd rather they went

13

elsewhere. She only mustered another barrage of adjectives, this time in a higher key. All the while the two men stood by dumbly looking at the floor. I didn't feel at my best in my tattered robe, curlers and crooked face, but I sort of expected one of them to either defend me somewhat or at least stop her. Neither moved a muscle until she had run out of insults. When she'd finished she walked haughtily to the bureau and picked up our car keys. Holding them out to Neal, she looked back over her shoulder for one last sweeping sneer at me and said, "Take me home." Neal obligingly took the keys and turned to the front door, Jack following behind them.

Pain and self pity got the best of me, and I couldn't stop the tears. I didn't want the girls to see, but I felt I had to go to them . . . do something. I swiped at my face the best I could and tried to blubber reassurances that everything was really all right, hurrying on to the subject of lunch and other distractions.

Strangely enough, the men came back in a couple of hours, Jack ducking straight up to the attic and Neal into bed. I was calm now . . . numb I guess . . . not just in my face. There didn't seem much I could add; surely Neal could see for himself what was wrong with that picture.

When he awoke, I gave him his dinner and went on with the routine . . . silently and dully, it's true, but blissfully not feeling anything. After awhile I could talk fairly cheerfully to the children and even direct mundane remarks or questions to Neal.

Fortunately for the sticky situation, he was called to work. Jack did not appear, so I could work on my feelings alone. Not that anything helpful occurred to me; I just didn't know what to do about it, and my physical condition seemed enough to cope with. Neal returned in the morning and got into bed just as I was getting out. Time was doing its healing work.

Late in the afternoon he came downstairs. He kindly enquired about my face, seemed genuinely contrite or perhaps just depressed, but at least respectful of something. By now, however, I was more concerned about Jack, who had not appeared in twenty-four hours.

"I suppose he could have gotten out while I was asleep, although I doubt it. You'd better go see, don't you think? What does he do when he needs the bathroom?"

"Out the window, I suppose."

"Neal! ... he does?" I tried to picture this and its implications, but had to admit it sounded possible for Jack. "Does he have any food up there?"

"I'll go investigate." Neal got up from his chair with a sigh. He couldn't understand these quirks of Jack's. With relief I soon heard them talking, and in a few minutes Neal reappeared.

"Dumb guy. He's sulking, I suppose, but anyway he says he's just fine and don't worry about him; he's reading and writing. He says he isn't hungry, but that can't be true. I'll take something up. Couldn't persuade him to come down for dinner." Neal snorted and shook his head. He'd never have any trouble this way or in accepting a meal. "Oh well, he'll get over it."

Monday morning I had an appointment with the clinic to start treatment on my face. When I returned, Jack had gone out. On my dressing table was our copy of *The Town and The City*. It certainly hadn't been there when I left. Mystified, I opened the cover for a clue, and inside, beneath the original inscription to me, Jack had written

"With the deepest apologies I can offer for the fiasco, the foolish tragic Saturday of Neal's birthday . . . all because I got drunk . . . Please forgive me, Carolyn, it'll never happen again. . . . "

So that was why he'd stayed upstairs: suffering with guilt and remorse. I was really touched, lifted and eager to show him all was certainly forgiven. Reading his note again, I felt his anguished sincerity. Not like Neal? Why could I look forward with pleasure to this situation, but not if it had been Neal? I supposed it was because I believed Jack when he said it would never happen again, and I'd learned it wasn't necessarily so with Neal. Even though I felt that Neal bore a good deal of the guilt in the recent episode, the idea of forgiving was still foreign. I might not retaliate, but this misdemeanor would simply join the ranks of all the others, ready to file in parade before him whenever I needed to remind him of my reasons for doubt. At least for the moment it was a relief to think I didn't feel it necessary and had learned enough not to grasp my only former solution of banishment.

So when Neal and Jack came home together that afternoon, we all had a shy, nervous but joyous new beginning. They brought beer and wine, and we set about dispelling the gloom. I had acquired an eye patch, since I couldn't close the one eye, and a paper-clip attached to a rubber band to hook my mouth to my ear so it wouldn't stray. Although this arrangement was a bit grotesque, we managed to find the humor in it. Neal poured oil on the troubled waters as only he could, being exuberant, witty and bombastic, keeping Jack and me laughing as I "whomped" up a big dinner while we guzzled beer and cheered ourselves and the children.

16

After dinner Jack opened the Tokay, but Neal preferred to finish the beer. Neither suggested going out; they appeared to be having a wonderful time, and for me it was a fiesta. Neal got out the tape recorder, and they got down to serious reminiscing. I gathered it was a treat for Jack as well; Neal rarely gave him his whole attention, and by so doing erased all Jack's remaining doubts about his welcome with us.

Chapter Three

Thus began a new life, or at least a new perspective on the old life, for me. When Jack wasn't at work or busy writing, he'd sit and talk to me, telling me of his childhood in Lowell, his mother's tenacity in working in the shoe factory, or about his sister Caroline's intolerance of him. Caroline was married, lived in North Carolina and had one son. Jack had a loyal affection for her, and felt it was an odd coincidence our names were so similar. She, however, felt Jack should get a job, support their mother and stop wasting his time playing around with writing. The publication of his first novel had quieted her temporarily, but when it wasn't a best seller, she renewed her original opinion.

Here with us he was trying to finish *On the Road* and find an agreeable publisher. Allen Ginsberg and a friend, Carl Solomon, who worked as an editor for a publisher uncle, were trying to help.

I had only read random passages in the manuscript; I was still too close to the actual events, and the more Neal enjoyed it, the more fearful I became that I'd feel the necessity to start something again. I had not heard the details of their trips, of course, and I was blissful in my ignorance. Jack was still writing scenes pertinent to it, and got really excited about the tape recorder, figuring he could do something unusual by copying exactly a taped spontaneous discussion. It looked as though *On the Road* might be an interminable highway. The new material I enjoyed reading, since it didn't reflect past revelations, and when Jack found he had an audience that felt he could do no wrong, he was happy to share his daily efforts. He still carried a little five-cent notebook in his shirt pocket wherever he went and wrote impressions or memories as he went along, usually typing them up within a few days. One of these I still have and cherish, although it was not a recent or local scene, but a remembrance of his Canadian relatives and his mother's girlhood. It delighted me and reminded me of Dickens. Although he told me many years later that he had typed it up and I could keep the notebook, I have not seen it published anywhere.

The liquor store was just around the corner, and Jack usually bought a small bottle of Tokay or Muscatel to sip late in the afternoon when he was tired of typing, or after dinner, sharing it with me. Occasionally I'd walk to the liquor store with him.

One day I stopped in alone to get some beer for "my husband." The proprietor said something about my husband's preference for sweet wine, and it wasn't till I was outside that I realized he meant Jack. I had to smile at the thought. It would seem that in at least in one neighborhood I led a double life. If they only knew how much trouble I had keeping one husband, let alone two.

One evening Neal came in dragging his feet and scowling. He had to pack to go to San Luis; he'd been called for a two week local hold-down. He didn't want to go, but there was no choice. He accepted the inevitable shortly, and managed some cheerfulness at dinner. We had to hurry, however, because his train departed in an hour. We were all brought down by this sudden development; each of us was uneasy. Jack and I were still somewhat self-conscious and shy when alone together, and the prospect of losing Neal as a buffer made us apprehensive.

This awkwardness was all that occurred to me, so I was

really embarrassed when Neal turned on the stair to wave goodbye to me and Jack, still seated at the table.

"Well, you know what they say . . . 'My best pal and my best gal.' Have a ball kiddies, so long." And he was off up the stairs. Jack and I nervously laughed it off as nothing, and when I got busy with the dishes, he bolted for the attic.

The more I thought of that remark, the madder I got, and it hurt, too. Well, maybe I was jumping to conclusions again; maybe he really did mean it as a joke.

The next two weeks Jack was gone a good deal, and hardly ever sat and talked to me. When he did agree to have dinner with me, it was so pleasant and delightful that we'd forget the circumstances for awhile; but then we'd come to and remember, ending up more nervous and uncomfortable each time. It may not be believed, but I'm sure neither of us seriously entertained the thought of following Neal's suggestion. This attitude wasn't "old-fashioned" on our parts, it just was one we held in common. It was more like the Golden Rule; we believed in loyalty and fidelity and had never thought of questioning it . . . yet.

When Neal returned it was with a great feeling of relief that we welcomed him. He seemed a little reserved our first evening at dinner, and I wondered if he supposed we had done as he no doubt would have in our shoes. When Jack had left us alone and gone upstairs, I asked Neal.

"Remember what you said when you left? That really hurt. Tell me, did you sincerely feel we should, or were you just trying to protect yourself in case it happened?"

He had started for the stairs and paused, shrugging his

shoulders.

"A little of both, I suppose . . . but actually, why not? I thought it would be fine." And up he went. Could he really be that cruel and unfeeling? I should know it by now, I thought dejectedly. Hadn't he "shared" Louanne . . . and how many others? Again I kept expecting I was different. Evidently not; just another of his women. It seemed far more of a rejection than just being deserted.

I was too sorry for myself and too busy mulling over his nature to think up solutions then, but when he came down to tell me he and Jack were going out, I got a vision of the future as an incessant repetition of the past, and I determined to find a way to change it. Once again, I seemed to shed another skin and broke the bonds of another conviction. *Okay, Neal dear, let's try it your way.* I felt slightly elated; an unaccustomed confidence, a coolness, a spurt of excitement . . . but fear, too. Never in my life had I known how to play those female games of deliberately setting out to attract a man. At least in this case it shouldn't require much aggression. A few manipulations of circumstances, perhaps, and just genuine appreciation. After all, Jack knew much better than I how Neal would be affected and how he would react. It was worth a try; it couldn't be worse than before.

Chapter Four

The very next evening, or one soon after, I made a few plans . . . nothing elaborate, nothing too unusual . . . but admittedly, I did some manipulating of circumstances.

It was easier than I had feared and I suppose I needn't have gone to any trouble at all. As it was it appeared as though I was simply asking Jack to have dinner with me when Neal was at work and the children asleep.

I made a pizza and a big salad I knew he liked, and I had bought wine, which I had to sample before he came downstairs to keep up my courage.

I had tried to make myself as pretty as I could without raising his suspicions. If I'd worn anything but my white shirt and jeans he would have wondered, but they were clean and ironed and my hair was soft and shiny and I smelled good from a little perfume.

Of course there was candlelight, too — I did that for Neal most of the time, or I guess for me, really, but I don't think Jack thought anything strange was going on. The wine calmed our nerves, and I liked listening to Jack and watching his gentle eyes and shy smiles, and he forgot himself and I forgot about plans and tricks and just enjoyed myself.

Right after we were through eating I knew I had to keep him there. He couldn't go back upstairs until I'd finished what I'd started; I'd never be able to do it all again. Of course I had the radio tuned to music I knew he liked, we both liked, and now I poured more wine in both glasses and walked to the couch, holding his out to him as I sat down so he'd see he had to come over there to get it. He did, and he lay back across the day-bed which we kept opened out, and closed his eyes, balancing his glass on his tummy, and hummed along with "My Funny Valentine." I looked down at him and didn't say anything. The silence grew thicker and warmer. "Do you remember when we danced together in Denver?" I asked. He turned his head toward me, smiling, and then he sat up, looking in my eyes with such a tender look. "Yeah," he said softly, "I wanted to take you away from Neal." He kept looking into my eyes but he stopped smiling. No further conniving was needed from me.

The relationship bloomed more rapidly than I had expected, but I was pleased my guilt was thus diminished. Jack was a tender and considerate lover, but, though I could be completely romantically in love with him, my heart still ached that it wasn't Neal. Also, my own compassion for anyone in Neal's position made me feel even more loving toward him, and I wavered in my resolve to teach him a lesson. I'd have sworn allegiance again in an instant, but worked at remembering his flippant words of indifference. I sincerely hoped some lasting good would come from this, but for now there was nothing to do but relax and enjoy it.

Although Jack and I found it easy to be extremely discreet when Neal was around, there was no concealing the change in us. Neal couldn't help but notice, yet the only evidence we had that he cared showed in an increased attentiveness to me.

The hope that my gamble would change the pattern of our lives was well founded. Everything appeared in a new light. I began a season of singing days and nights, I was a *part* of all they did now and I felt like the star of the show. Besides, I felt I was a real contributor for once. My housework and baby care had a *purpose*; it was needed and appreciated. I was functioning as a female, and my men were men. It may have taken two of them to complete the picture generally relegated to one, but so much the better. They were such different types; how lucky could a girl get? Each was being himself, and I served whichever was in residence according to their individual requirements. If they were both home at once, Neal usually slept and Jack wrote. Jack tried to go out and leave the real husband and wife alone if Neal was up and about. Jack, like me, felt Neal's and my marriage came first. We both deeply believed in the institution, and neither of us looked on this new arrangement as an attempt to destroy that bond. We never really thought to define what we were doing, but as peace and joy reigned as a result, we let it go at that.

Jack and I never made love when Neal was home. At first they kept out of each other's way because they didn't know exactly what was happening, but after awhile, when no big dramatic scenes took place, and Neal saw that Jack and I weren't going to love him any less, everyone relaxed, drew together, and were as discreet and kind as possible.

Jack and I didn't have all that much of a mad passionate affair going anyway. He wasn't half as interested in sex as Neal; Jack was more affectionate and intellectual, and when he was working nights we didn't have many opportunities to be together.

We did make love on his bed in the attic sometimes when the children took their naps and Neal was on a train, but only when Jack asked or invited me. I remember with pleasure the warm sun from his window lying across us like a blanket, and the smell of unfinished wood.

At the dinner table both Neal and Jack would talk to me, tell me their adventures. The only time there was trouble was when Neal would get a mean streak, turn all of his attention to me and treat Jack like he wasn't there. Then Jack would sulk, and if Neal were mean enough Jack would get up and stamp upstairs. Neal would construe that as his, Neal's, having "won," so he'd call after Jack and beg him to come back and make it up. It was just a game to Neal, or a little bit of getting even, and he liked that kind of challenge to his ego. He liked feeling that he was the best man around. He always became a better lover and put more into a relationship when it was threatened; maybe that's why he shared all his women, it made it more exciting for him. If you were the faithful kind he'd have to bring men to you himself, as he did to me later on, trying to stir things up, and I never got over being shocked.

Chapter Five

While I performed my household duties the men would read each other excerpts from their writing in progress or bring out Spengler, Proust or Shakespeare to read aloud, accompanied by energetic discussions and appraisals. Neal always had the radio going as well, so digressions and interruptions ensued to dig a musician or arrangement and discuss that. I was happy just listening to them and filling their coffee cups. Yet I never felt left out. They'd address remarks to me and include me in the group with smiles, pats and requests for opinions or to moderate an argument.

They still made forays together in search of tea or to buy groceries but were never gone very long. If Neal was at home sleeping, Jack and I sometimes took walks together down to Aquatic Park or to Chinatown. Spring was beginning to soften the air, but the wind could still be brisk. Jack found a wonderful old-fashioned Chinese restaurant on a little street adjacent to St. Francis Park that served great bowls of steaming won ton soup for thirty-five cents and equally delectable bowls of fried rice for twenty-five. Often we warmed ourselves thus and then sat on a bench in the park.

The times when Neal and I were alone were happier too. We had the children's progress to enjoy together; we discussed the economics of the household and other such parental concerns. I was able to be especially affectionate to him now, and he accepted my expressions of love in better grace.

One night Jack went out alone but came back in a few minutes and tried to get Neal and I as excited as he was about having discovered that Joan Crawford was only a block away making a movie. For some reason neither Neal or I wanted to go, and Jack went back out with his notebook. Hours later he returned and stayed up all night writing "Joan Crawford in the Fog." Years later, when it was published, he called her Joan Rawshanks, but the next day when he read it to us it was only Joan Crawford, and I was always sorry afterward I hadn't gone with him.

From Jack's wanderings alone he collected some new friends, and they would visit us, widening my horizons still further. There was a diverse assortment of men and boys. As a rule he'd take them up to his room so as not to inconvenience me, and I didn't get to know many very well, but occasionally Neal was home and would invite them down to the kitchen. There were students, musicians, artists, poets, mostly would-bes, and sometimes the kind of philosophers that seemed forerunners of the Hippies. One such was particularly puzzling to me. He was a cadaverous boy, afire with a new discovery: "the absolute answer to all the world's ills." He called it Dianetics, and it has since become more well known as Scientology. However, I was then totally unfamiliar with this kind of esoteric thought. I couldn't understand a word he said, and when I'd look at his desperately poor condition I'd feel that he was an unconvincing advertisement.

Charlie, whom Neal brought home one afternoon, was a steward on a passenger liner, and I suppose Neal must have met him on one of his expeditions in search of tea. He lived in the Tenderloin area with some pretty basic characters and had a daughter whom he housed with one woman or another of dubious genre. It was a situation that frightened me, and although we tried to help the child from time to time, I was out of my depth.

Charlie was a tiny thing, only about five feet tall with a round shining face. His age was difficult to assess, but I guessed it to be in the middle thirties. He was always cheerful and bubbling and loved to join the boys for blasting.

One evening they got together with tea, wine, the tape recorder and a variety of instruments: recorders, wooden flutes, maracas and an old harmonica. Jack never stopped drumming, whether or not an actual drum was available. He did very well on the bottoms of assorted cooking pans or oatmeal cartons. To my great relief the saxaphone and bugle were not included this time.

I declined to indulge in the tea but was interested in studying its effect on them. They had a riotous good time, sometimes hung up on their musical improvisations, sometimes on the replay of same, but mostly howling with laughter and appreciation over what they apparently considered an inordinate display of brilliant wit. Charlie was not in their league intellectually — his mind was inclined to run to the earthy and his comments were usually connected with sex. I decided the tea was not responsible for this exceptional cleverness, but only for making them think it was so. Quite the contrary seemed the case to me; nothing they expressed showed any really heightened perception; they were so high dumb things just didn't sound dumb. After a short time, I was content to bid them a bored good night and retire. Jack later inserted his transcription of the tapes of one of these conversations into his novel *Visions of Cody*.

One night two or three friends came over with a new

28

kick. Neal was all excited and the atmosphere took on an expectant and awesome feel. They had brought peyote, and Neal and Jack had never had it. Explicit directions were given and followed; all theories and reported results reviewed. Neal watched, leaning on the table with eyes aglow as the friend carefully chopped up the lobes of cactus as finely as its toughness would allow.

"Well, how do you take it, man? Cook it?" Neal was impatient.

"No, no . . . just eat it . . . chew it up. Only trouble is, it makes you nauseated at first, but if you can keep it down . . . wow . . . like you've never seen such colors . . . technicolor visions."

I knew then this was an experience I would forever have to forego. When I weighed the thought of purposely causing oneself to be nauseated against such possible "visions," the visions lost out. I'd have to live with my own feeble imagination. All such external administrations to the psyche make me apprehensive, but I squared my shoulders and decided I'd stick around and be able to function normally if anyone required help.

Each participant ceremoniously chewed a tablespoon or two full of the grey-green mound and either sat on the couch to await results or ascended to the attic. I watched and waited. All was quiet. Extremely. I couldn't tell when they ceased struggling with the rising nausea and became deep in their dreams. Since dim lighting appeared to part of the ritual, I went to bed to read, still remaining alert to any signs of distress. No emergency arose, and no one cared to communicate their sensations that night, so I gave it up and went to sleep.

Even the next day, my efforts at drawing out some

descriptions of their wondrous experience were mostly futile. Neither Jack nor Neal could remember anything particularly startling or revelatory. It may just have been that they couldn't find words to match, unlikely in Jack's case, but it seemed the deepest impression remaining with them was the nausea. Neal's stomach was so sensitive anyway, he had lost the first dose and made himself repeat the ordeal. I doubt he was as enthusiastic on the second try. Nevertheless, they kept some peyote in the refrigerator and wrote to Allen in more glowing terms, so he requested a sample for himself.

Chapter Six

In the first couple of months since Jack's arrival my self-esteem expanded as I found acceptance as a desirable companion both mentally and physically. I decided to go along with Jack's expectation that I would now join him, with or without Neal, on evenings out. It was gratifying to find he thought of me as a necessary adjunct, yet I started out still somewhat timidly, conditioned by past outings with Neal. Besides, the bohemian scene now was less compatible to me than when I'd been younger. The people were more intense; it seemed they took themselves so seriously. Could it be the drugs and their illegality? Few seemed just to have *fun* anymore. There was an aura of suspicion and defensiveness, but maybe I was reflecting my own fears.

One night Jack had heard of a "pay the rent" party in a loft down near the docks. Everyone was expected to donate money unless he was a musician, in which case admission was free. Both Jack and Neal considered themselves musicians, and they heartily upheld each other's claim to the title. Unfortunately, each was without instrument. Neal took along a recorder for emergency proof, but Jack decided to explain he had just arrived from New York and had left his drums behind. Surely he could prove his prowess on borrowed bongos. *Everybody* had bongos.

We arrived early, the better to bluff. The "loft" was a huge second storey over a warehouse. Its appearance was made as inviting as the bareness allowed. The wood floor was clean, a few mattresses were arranged in L's or facing one another or against the walls, covered with paisley or colored cotton spreads. Numerous candles made arcs of golden light, and hangings of colored burlap separated kitchen and bathroom areas. A patch or two of colorful shag rugs warmed the seating areas. The one small Franklin stove in the corner was bravely blinking and puffing, but it was a losing battle three feet beyond its perimeter, and I decided to keep on my coat.

When we arrived there was only the hostess, a young thing in a long sack-like dress, and three or four transient males. Neal charged right in, overwhelming the timid girl with a look of stern authority, leaving the niceties to Jack and me. Jack politely and sincerely explained their qualifications for admittance and asked if there might be a spare pair of bongos on hand he could use. The girl hesitated, not altogether convinced, and cast nervous glances in Neal's direction as he strode arrogantly about, sizing up the place. Something must have told her she was out of her depth, so she grudgingly pointed Jack toward a pad midway in the hall, beside which was a beautiful pair of bongo drums.

Jack bustled seriously over and inspected them.

"Hey," he came back to the hostess, "they're awful loose."

"They haven't been used for awhile. Just heat them . . . hold them over that gas burner for a minute; they'll shrink." She looked at Jack even more dubiously. He did as she suggested.

Since I wasn't a musician by any stretch of fantasy, nor had I contributed to the rent, I tried to be as inconspicuous as possible and melt into the limited scenery. Neal had disappeared, so I pretended to look for him. I went out the front door. On the outside stair landing and from the depths below came excited voices and considerably more activity than inside. I heard Neal among them and realized he must be conducting his perpetual search for tea. He wouldn't want me there, so I wandered back inside, trying to keep an expectant party face. I was alerted by Jack furtively motioning me to come to him. He was seated on a mattress, his back to the hostess and doorway, bending over the drums. I sat down on the opposite mattress. "How you doin?"

"Look what I've *done*," he moaned, his face contorted in dismay. He tilted up the drums part way, enough for me to see the charred and blackened skin around a two-inch hole in one of the drum heads. "My God," he whispered, "they were practically new . . . I didn't notice the flame was so high . . . the blue top of it was invisible, I swear it. Jesus, what'll I do?"

I shook my head. What *could* we do? Even offering to pay for them was no good. I knew his remorse was genuine and acute; he loved instruments and was never careless with them. It was too painful to even think of trying to explain it to all these strangers.

"We'd just better go before it's discovered. I hate to do it, but they're already hostile toward us, and without the means to replace them . . . what a shame. Poor Jack. Come on."

He had already risen, and with a bravado of nonchalance, tried not to hurry to the door. I followed suit. By now a few more guests were arriving, so the hostess was busy talking to them and sorting out the musicians. So far I'd seen no one offer cash. As we escaped through the door, I silently wished her luck with the rent. Outside we fairly flew down the stairs, clutching Neal as we passed

33

him from a group of bearded men. Our frowns stopped his forming question, and he took his hasty leave, following us at a trot.

On the way home in the car, we enlightened Neal and all stayed glumly silent till we had sat down with a cup of hot coffee. Little by little the whole scene struck us as funny. Neal tried unsuccessfully to conceal his feeling that this was typical of Jack and instead covered it by telling other stories of times they'd had in similar tragic circumstances, exaggerating and gesticulating till we were all holding our sides. Neal had scored, so his evening was a success; Jack relieved his guilt by blaming the hostess, the loose drums and the invisible flame, and I was happier to be safe at home. The only disappointed person was the baby-sitter who hadn't earned enough money.

Another night Jack asked me to accompany him to a party, this time with Neal's benediction, as Neal couldn't leave the phone and was content to sleep until his work call should come. The party was in a private apartment, and there were four or five other couples. The owner and host was Jordan Belson, a talented artist and photographer. The group had been especially invited to view a film he had just completed. The room was small but attractive and comfortable. The assembled company formed a semi-circle in the seating, and Jack and I were at the midway point. At the upper open end was the movie screen. I had struck up a conversation with a delightful girl on my right and was intent on listening to her, not noticing that two joints of marijuana had been lit and were being passed down each side of the circle . . . each ending with me. So as not to seem prudish, I had been absent-mindedly taking puffs as each joint was handed me, not realizing I was getting two tokes to everyone else's one. Soon the film was begun, and I was even more unaware of my surroundings. The film was the first of its kind I'd ever seen, and I was fascinated. Belson had animated line drawings and paint splotches to mambo music. It was totally abstract and delightful. I didn't want it to end, but when it did, so did I. I couldn't move. I sat absolutely rigid, unable to control a single muscle . . . "stoned" came literally to my mind. So that was what it meant. My God, what was I to do? Rising panic made me icy cold, as well. It seemed an eon before Jack turned to me and said something requiring an answer. He put his hand on my arm. Thank God, I could speak! His touch broke the spell. He turned away again, perfectly calmly, having noticed nothing unusual. Could that be? I thought everyone in the room must be aware of my helpless condition. I wanted to tell Jack, but now I was blocked again . . . what to say? The panic returned. Never had I been so frightened.

The party was breaking up. Jack and the others were moving about, collecting coats and making farewells. I just sat there. Somebody was bound to notice. Every nerve and fiber of my being was intent on keeping my mind alert and "there." With extreme effort, I found I could lean forward, change position, try and appear cool, but I didn't dare try to stand. Jack came over and held out his hand, my coat on his other arm. When I saw I was responding by reaching for his hand, and when we touched I could rise, relief swept over me. I was all right.

Not quite. "Jordan wants to know if we can drive him over to Columbus . . . I told him it was right on our way,

OK?" I heard what Jack was saying. It sounded so simple. DRIVE, I thought . . . good grief . . . how could I DRIVE? The panic rose, but I had to go on. I went through the motions of climbing into my coat and holding Jack's arm, and got out the door and down the stairs, feeling as though I were floating in a surrealistic dream. Did I really appear normal to him? Jack acted as though I did. I started to tell him I couldn't drive when I remembered Neal's original instructions during my first experience with tea: "Remember, you can always do anything you have to do." I grasped these words, repeating them over and over as we made our way to the car. I didn't know what the men were doing nor talking about. And sure enough, I drove Jordan where he wanted to go, and right on through the traffic and busy streets up the hill to home. I thanked God, or whatever was responsible, but I also needed no urging to resolve that that was to be my last tea party. Neal was just leaving for work when we reached the house, so I said nothing of my experience to either of them, wanting to talk to Neal about it more privately. Just to be close to Jack's naturally reassuring presence was enough for now.

Chapter Seven

Since Jack's arrival, Allen had been writing more often; it was plain to see he envied his friends being together without him.

> Last night I had my eyes closed, sleeping (half asleep) and thinking about Neal's birthday, which led me to think of my own in 6 months . . . I will be 26 like Neal. It has been occurring to me often that years now seem shorter, more fast to fly. At 26 we are almost 30 actually, and I woke with a powerful knock of awareness at my heart, my eyes flew open. I saw time flying like an enormous bird. We are getting to our age of most power, our peak. I feel older and clearer than I ever did . . . though at the same time more irretrievably isolated in the huge dream of the world. I don't really see much future, since by now I should be more *connected* to outside things, like $ and society. Whatever I want, I still am not what I wanted to be . . . none of the many kinds of things I wanted to be . . . and perhaps will not be. The opening of the eyes goes on.

He wrote long poems, stories about everyone he knew and repeated everyone else's stories to him. We enjoyed taking turns reading his letters aloud and discussing them. It might occupy a whole morning or afternoon. Allen also kept us posted on his efforts toward the literary output of his friends and what was happening with Bill Burroughs in Mexico.

> Burroughs has been writing. He is lonely. Write to him. Bill says "Meanwhile things seem kind of

dreary around here. I want to get the case settled and clear out."* His kids have been claimed by respective grandparents.

Jack, please write New Directions a short note telling them how much you like Bill's book, recommending it for prose and archive value, and telling, as I did in 6 page letter, it's a great book. I have revised the version Bill sent up 2 weeks ago... smoother now, not so weird Reichian. If Laughlin no want, we'll peddle it to cheap paper covered 25¢ Gold Medal or Signet Books, like "I, Mobster."

Carl is serious about Neal's manuscript. Neal, get to it, honey lamb. He'll give you money, and you are a great man.

How I miss both of you and wish I were there with you so that we could share hearts again. I know I am hard to get along with and proud; I insulted Jack before he left and felt many twinges of sadness ...I only hope that you are not laughing at me when I am here away from your warmth. Write me. I think about you all the time, and have no one to talk to as only we can talk.

How or when will I ever hear your records? I sit here and my soul lacks you Neal and you Jack. I hope my ship goes your way to Frisco. I don't want ever to fade from your minds.

Love, Allen

Put a kiss and a tear
In a letter,
And I'll open and cry
Over you.

---

*A reference to the shooting of Burroughs' wife.

Put a sperm and a wink
On the paper,
And I'll come when I read,
I'm so blue.

Put a throb of your heart
In "yours truly",
With your names writ in blood
"Neal and Jack:,

And I'll open my palm
With my penknife,
And send you a bucket-
Full back.

Done in 3 minutes
A.G.

Jack was becoming depressed by the painful hassle with his ex-wife and her efforts to get money from him. He had given whatever advance he'd received from the publishers to his mother and didn't make enough in the baggage room to give J the agreed amount. He just felt like running. We tried to sympathize, but the mention of her name made him angry. Allen offered sensible, fatherly advice:

Carl upset you still starving, and that your mother keeps your money. Why don't you use it yourself? You are in a worse hole than your mother. I spoke to lawyer about wife and he said either change your address to keep safe or send money (from another postal town) according to agreement. If want to stay in country safe and without anxiety, that's only way. You're letting yourself get too unnecessarily tangled up in sad fate. Let's figure a way to clean things up before it gets further, makes writing paranoid and life lousy. It's strictly situation, external, not absolute and fixed fate for you unless you *leave* it be fixed fate. Am not being analytic-moral. None of us are fast and strong enough to battle society forever really, it's too sad and grey. Just felt you were feeling too crazy lately and am putting out friend-hand. Must not let situation drift to intolerability. We got too much else to do besides suffer.

Much to my delight and surprise, Allen even included a note to me, at last acknowledging my existence.

Dear Mrs. Cassady:
How is you, after all. I know I've always been beat in your imagination, but I never meant you no harm personally. In fact, as I see things now, I think maybe you been through the mill bad, always been sorry I contributed to the privation; but in extenuation my part was very small in fact it was jess part of everybodys fate. Too bitter to forgive? I hope not.
Take care of the children (that means Jack too and Neal) as everybody will ultimately be saved, including you. I'm sure, in fact I think that's happened to the Cassadys already, however much as Jack says Neal is half deaf and walks around unlistening like a Zombie and is a most unreassuring character, always seemed he was listening to his sores.
I plan no imminent invasion of Frisco but would like to some day and hope I will be welcome to you and we can be friends. You always seem alright to

40

me. Jack likes you but is afraid of you. (You know?).
I wonder how you feel about him.

Yours,
Allen the Stranger

I was overjoyed to be thus recognized officially as a
worthy member of the clan and hoped to revive Allen's
friendship as I had known it in Denver. I hastened to
answer him warmly and received a reassuring reply:

> Much thanks for your letter. Didn't expect to be
> so well received either. So that disperses that cloud.
> Was Jack's tip too; he not so dumb, with other
> people's female notions. Will arrive in Frisco by
> underground railway someday. Would like to come
> not beat and add to everybody else's problems and
> be dependent, though it's sweet to be accepted as
> dependent if I can't make it otherwise. Would be
> interested know your process of changes of love and
> thought. Don't realize too much of yr. interior of
> last years except by conjecture. Thank you for child
> name. Never got the idea from W.C. Fields that you
> had anything to do with it, but now that you
> mention it does sound sort of inevitable that you
> might have had some hand in naming yr. own
> children. Yipe! Consider my letters henceforth
> addressed to you too. Would it be possible have my
> epistles (like St. Paul) read in state at dinner table in
> front of the children of the Church? Constantinople
> here needs me so can't get to Rome temporarily, am
> waiting for a Word. Understood your letter.
>
> Thanks. Shy. Allen.

It appeared kind-hearted Jack had bridged the gap, a
thing Neal had never thought to do.

41

Chaper Eight

My blooming self-confidence developed a step further into a daring hitherto unknown in my sheltered experience. The railroad was slow, but Neal was fortunate to be able to "bump" a younger man and hold down a daily freight local. It looked like a long run, but he'd make much less money than on the extra board, so I decided to try and help the financial situation by looking for a job at night, something simple, fun and untaxing, something I could quit without feeling irresponsible. I knew being a waitress was out; I'd nearly fallen apart trying to do it in college. I scoured the want-ads and found it: a hat check girl was needed at the St. Francis Hotel. Surely I could manage that. It sounded perfect. Next morning I marched down to the hotel and talked to the personnel man. It was educational but discouraging. If I were looking for full time work, he said, forget it. This was only good as an extra job; all the girls had other jobs since the pay was far too low to be sufficient for support.

"What about tips?"

"No go. They have to turn in all their tips to the management. Cigarette girls, flower girls; none of them get to keep their tips." This was a real revelation to me. "What a weird system; why do people tip them, then? How come nobody knows or the girls don't just say, 'No thanks'? How could the management ever know how much they'd collected?" I caught sight of the man's amused expression and ceased.

"There is one concession that lets the girls keep the tips. Camera girl in a club. Their pay is insignificant, too, I understand, but at least they can work up the tips. Why don't you try that?"

This wasn't nearly as appealing to me. It involved selling, and I'd already discarded that idea, but I was in it this far, so I might as well investigate. He gave me the name of the man to see and directed me to the International Settlement in North Beach. This dazzling block of nightclubs was neither a "settlement" nor "International," yet everyone knew it was the last remnants of the Barbary Coast in San Francisco.

Mustering all my courage, I walked under the archway across the beginning of the block that spelled out its name in lights and headed for the photo booth. It was like a carnival street with overtones of a side show, and the open area I sought was ablaze with lights and lures to entice the passing servicemen to have their pictures taken. I found the boss in his small office behind the dark-room.

He looked the Hollywood prototype for just such a position: fleshy, coarse features with black hair and eyes and the built-in cigar. I became even more timid under the scrutiny of those hard, bulging eyes. What was I *doing* toying with the underworld? I was anything but tough and aggressive and certainly not stimulated by danger. Was I insane or simply stupid? Too late now. He was rapidly outlining in a dull monotone the routine and duties I was expected to perform. There wasn't any salary as such; I'd get a percentage of every order plus the tip. He looked me over dubiously. "Joe will give you a camera and show you how it works." He waved the cigar in the direction of the dark-room and left.

My territory consisted of three supper clubs: a small Mexican cafe, The Xochimilco, which served excellent food and had a good combo but very few patrons; The Beige Room in the next block, whose floor show consisted of female impersonators (I was not allowed to take any pictures during the shows); and the third was in Chinatown, which required my hiring a cab to reach. It boasted "exotic dancers," but was frequented almost entirely by regular customers that I was forcefully forbidden to approach. When an occasional soldier or sailor (the uniform was the only way I could be sure they weren't one of the regulars) did wander into the place, they rarely wanted photographs. A further trial here was the fact that the dark-room was beyond the kitchen, necessitating my passing tables heaped with aromatic Chinese food I wasn't allowed to sample.

The dark-room for the first two was in the Sinaloa, about three blocks away. This had long been a popular club with elaborate Mexican floor shows and bands. The camera girl there was an old-timer, and she informed me that all the new girls got my "beat" because it was almost impossible to take any pictures in any of the three places. It was therefore a good way for the boss to test any exceptional talent for the profession among the newcomers without loss to himself. No wonder he hadn't quizzed me on qualifications nor laid down any rules of conduct. The Sinaloa girl had started this way herself but now was able to stay in one location and make good money. As I watched her techniques for soliciting photographs from reluctant guests, I knew I'd never be a success at this.

Ah well, I'd hang on awhile; it was exciting finding out what it was like being a "night person," and my theater background led me to enjoy being behind any scene.

I dug out some of the first clothes I had bought in San Francisco years before which had been too dressy for my needs up to now. This job required that I be as flashy as possible, including high heels. Whenever I took a photograph I'd have to walk the 3 blocks to the Sinaloa to get it developed, and if I made a mistake, which I frequently did at first, it meant running back and forth for retakes before the people either left or got disgusted. As I recall, it also rained more nights than not, so maintaining glamor was an additional challenge.

Neal and Jack seemed content with their babysitting obligation and the time alone together. I worked from six until two, but often they were still up when I'd get home. We'd have a cup of coffee while I unwound, and they'd encourage me to tell them my adventures for the night. "So what's new in the sinful city tonight, eh?"

"Well, you'll never believe it. I had a huge fight with the owner of The Beige Room. It's this woman, see? She's only about thirty, and I thought she was the hostess. Well, anyway, I took a picture during one of the shows and I hear this scream from back by the bar and out she stomps, crimson with rage."

"I thought you weren't allowed to take pictures duing the shows."

"I'm not, but this wasn't technically during a show. Geez, I asked everybody, but everybody. This guy was just playing the piano, and I asked him what he thought. Then I asked a guy fixing the lights; I asked waiters, everyone. Everyone said sure, go ahead. Since I never get any pictures there, I just had to. Do you realize they actually run Grey Line tours to this place? So there's just lots of potential customers. Ha. Every little businessman and his wife from Topeka draw back in alarm at my suggestion. 'Not HERE!' they shriek. They're being so devilishly wicked, but they don't want the folks at home to know . . . even when I tell them I'll put it in a plain wrapper. Honestly."

"You can be sure they're gonna TELL the folks back home, though, that they went to a place like that," Jack laughed, and Neal shook his head, adding his "Yeah, yeah, but what about the fight?"

"Oh, yes. Well, like I said, I let fly with the flash and instantly I hear this shriek, 'Stop that! What do you think you're doing?' It took me a minute to realize she meant me, and I was devastated at being made so conspicuous in front of all those people. But I walked up to her, trying to compose myself and be as calm as possible. I explained the whole episode, pointing out all the people I'd asked for permission. 'You didn't ask *me*! She's still hollering at the top of her voice, and I began to get a bit heated myself. 'So, who are you?' I retorted, 'I OWN this place.' Her eyes were blazing. 'Now, how was I to know that? I thought you were the head waiter.' I meant to say 'hostess' but it didn't come to me, and I knew it couldn't be maitre d'. By now I'm shaking with the whole unpleasantness, so I told her I was sorry, but she's still afire, so I just walked out. I expect I'll hear from the boss . . . but, you know, it was kinda fun. Me. Imagine me doing a thing like that."

"Wal, I dunno, my dear . . . I can remember a time or two . . . "

"Never mind, Dad. They weren't public."

"What are the shows like?" Jack wanted to know. "Is it like Finnochio's . . . where I've never been?"

46

"I suppose so. I've never been either. I always thought flaunting homosexuality like that was kinda tragic. But, you know, I understand a whole lot better now. The shows are really good . . . I mean, in good taste, actually. The star is a comedian and hilarious. The only part I'm not too sold on is when he gets off on the guys in drag. Then he gets pretty bitter. One night he actually pointed out two in the audience who were really done up and I must admit awfully swishy, and he says with great disgust, 'THATS what people think WE are.' I was embarrassed. But, most of the show is real talent, and that's what they emphasize. One girl . . . guy is a beautiful singer; he . . . she sings semi-classics, and there's another that sings popular ballads, also marvelous. They have piano players . . . well, yes, they do have one who strips, but he's funny, and they make it all very light-hearted. No, really, a more professional show I've never seen anywhere, or better performers. I'd never have believed it.But I just can't think of them as men. They come and sit with me between numbers; show me their expensive gloves and hose, and . . . honestly, they aren't built anywhere like a man . . . well, sorry, I'm not qualified to say that . . . but hips, arms, everywhere else . . . feminine characteristics. Hey . . . I know . . . you should both come down for a drink some night . . . why don't you? They sit and size up each new man that comes in and speculate whether he would or wouldn't. I'd love to hear what they thought about you two . . . ha, ha. . . . "I was delighted with the picture I projected mentally. Neither of them seemed pleased.

A few nights after my blow-up with the owner of The Beige Room, one of the drummers thought I should learn to mambo, and since there were only a couple of customers, he started the juke box and proceeded to demonstrate with me on the little dance floor. It was the only time I saw my boss since starting the job. He had to pick that moment. He didn't say anything about any of my activities, but I realized as well as he that I was not getting anywhere. My nightly take averaged about a dollar and a half, so one night when I made a five dollar tip at the Chinese club, I decided to quit while I was ahead.

Meanwhile, the men were also getting tired of this routine. Jack was disgruntled by continuing pressure from J and battles with the publishers. He had written quite a lot more that was to be part of *On the Road* and felt he'd done enough. He was anxious to go to Mexico, talking longingly of the peace and simplicity of the life he envisioned.

In the light of the past months of comparative compatibility and serenity with Neal, I felt our married life had built a firm foundation and I let my thoughts return to plans for family life around the old conventional patterns that had formed my own.

In this regard, I felt the need of a solidifying tie with the grandparents, who had never seen our children, but had consistently shown their exceptional interest in them. So, we decided to go to Tennessee and visit them, giving Neal an opportunity to see the farm, as well. Of course, Neal was ready to travel at the drop of an excuse, and he thought it appropriate I should get to go on at least one Road with him. Besides, I hadn't had any sort of vacation for five years. On top of everything, maybe he could find his father somewhere along the way.

There was no doubt now, the trip was an absolute necessity, not just pleasure. I plunged into plans. He could take a month off the railroad, which was slow anyway. We'd take all the baby food and most of our own, spell each other driving and keep the motels to a minimum. We'd drive Jack as far as Nogales and thus start him out on his way to Mexico.

Chapter Nine

Everything worked out beautifully. We took the back seats out of the station wagon and covered the floor with mattresses, John's crib mattress fitting perfectly across the back and leaving room enough between it and the front seat for both little girls to sleep. Our few bags lined the sides providing back rests in the daytime. Jack had only a sea bag, and the food was boxed. There was a surprising amount of room.

Jack took a nostalgic farewell of his attic nook, but he and I had no opportunity for a private talk. We'd all been bravely minimizing the separation by making happy plans for reuniting in Mexico. It somehow seemed accepted that we would all share a home somewhere, at least for part of each year.

The girls were so excited, they wanted to ride in front with daddy, so Jack and I crawled in the back with John, and sat crossways, facing each other. It was somewhat cramped for two adults, but this suited our romantic feelings. We lapsed into a silent reverie, realizing the imminent separation. We could make no move toward each other without feeling sorry for Neal, so communication had to be entirely by longing looks and an occasional electric touch of knees. The tension was near unbearable by the time we reached Santa Barbara, yet it was a satisfying romantic agony.

We stayed the first night with Neal's younger sister in Santa Barbara and then headed for Los Angeles, where Neal was able to locate an older sister and two older brothers. We visited from house to house, all of them being very cordial.

By dinner time, when I realized Neal planned to stay, I was becoming extremely uncomfortable about being a party to what looked to me like another of his con games. I fretted to Jack, who explained to me in his kindly way that I should forget it; people loved Neal and didn't mind his giving them the chance to give. Still, I wasn't so sure this branch of the family was all that fond of Neal, and to just arrive with three adults and three children.... But my efforts at expressing these fears to the relatives were silenced; they made us all feel most welcome and certainly seemed sincere. At length I held my peace, content to lie on the floor near Jack and watch the late, late show, the first television I had actually ever seen in a home.

All the next day's drive I sat in the back, giving my attention to the girls and the sights we were passing, letting Jack and Neal have a last time together too. I had to smile thinking what a different "Road" it was this time to the ones they'd shared before. It didn't sound as though the family presence was dampening their ardor in the least; in fact it seemed to add to their pleasure if ever we passed a place they could remember and tell me about, embellishing the story to ever greater glories.

We drove all night across the desert. A beautiful night ... all of us happy and in tune ... our last night together. We three sat in the front seat and listened to radio plays while the children slept. Neal got so emotionally involved in "The Whistler" Jack and I had to laugh and repeatedly remind him it was only a play. He probably was putting us on, but I got a little nervous, he seemed to take it so seriously. Later we all peered into the panorama of glittering stars above us, while Neal astounded and intrigued us with a complete and detailed discourse on the constellations, their history and meaning.

"Whenever did you learn all that?" we asked together. "I didn't know you knew anything about astronomy."

"Ah knows everthing about everthing . . . how many times do Ah have to tell yew?"

As the morning drew near, I let my head rest on Jack's shoulder, and although he patted my hair or pretended he was asleep and didn't notice, it was apparent very soon that it made him too uncomfortable, so I changed position. Funny guys. But I didn't care; I loved 'em, and I relished my last few hours with them both, counting my blessings.

Early in the morning we reached Nogales. We drove to the border and parked the car. It was grey and dreary; the weather, the town and now our moods.

"Aw, come on. Can't you have one last beer with me?" Jack was standing forlornly with his sea bag on his shoulder. Neal jumped out of the car. "Sure, man," and I followed him, careful not to wake the children. We had parked just outside a white-walled cafe, so we could see the car through the window. Inside was one large bare room, a bar running most of its length, and few metal tables scattered about. Hardly a place to cheer us, drinking a beer that early and before breakfast helped a little. Though we spoke little, Jack's thoughts were hopping from the Mexico ahead to the past with us, but after a few brave attempts at cheery conversation, he too fell silent. I rather imagine Neal was wishing he were Jack, but he gave no indication to that effect and only mentioned we could all be there with him in a few more months.

Neal was soon anxious to travel on, and we said our corny goodbyes and promises and waved till we'd lost sight of the lonely figure by the border fence.

Chapter Ten

As it was, the improved feelings Neal and I recaptured with Jack's presence had no permanence without Jack as the catalyst. My reactions on the trip back were in the same pattern as before, and though we both tried to hang on to the peace we'd been enjoying the past few months, we had no knowledge of its foundation. We were still vulnerable in the same ways. It distressed me greatly to find our life still threatened, and I continually searched out its cause and cure. Now, too, I could add another worry: we hadn't heard a word from Jack in over a month. Had I split everyone asunder? Neal was no help; he had come down with a thud after all the activity and the return to the old routine. His depressed state either made him dodge talking to me about it or he'd be flip and discouraging.

So I turned to Allen, whom I now felt was my friend, too, and he *had* invited me to reveal my "interior." I poured out my anxieties and asked his guidance. Graciously, he gave his attention and thoughtful consideration to my plea:

Jack's attitude:

a) As I haven't got all his letters here, I'll send on an anthology of statements apropos his relations with Neal when I assemble them. What *I* think about it is, Jack loves Neal platonically (which I think is a pity, but maybe about sex I'm "projecting" as the analysts say), and Neal loves Jack, too. The fact is that Jack is very inhibited, however. However, also sex doesn't define the whole thing.

b) Jack still loves Neal no less than ever.

c) Jack ran into a blank wall which everybody understands and respects in Neal, including Jack and Neal. It upset and dispirited Jack, made him feel lonely and rejected and like a little brother whose questions the older brother wouldn't answer.

d) Jack loves Carolyn also, though obviously not with the same intensity and power as he loves Neal, and this is acceptable and obvious considering all parties involved, their history together, how much they knew each other and how often they lived thru the same years and crises. Jack is full of Carolyn's praises and nominates her to replace Joan Burroughs as Ideal Mother Image, Madwoman, chick and ignu. The last word means a special honorary type post-hip intellectual. Its main root is ignoramus from the mythology of W.C.Fields. Jack also says Carolyn beats Dusty for Mind.

e) Jack said nothing about sleeping with you in his letters.

f) Jack thinks Neal is indifferent to him, however only in a special way, as he realizes how good Neal has been to him and that Neal really loves him; but they couldn't communicate I guess. However, he would love to live all together with everybody in Mexico, I believe. He would claim right to treat Neal as a human being and hit him on the breast with balloons. I will transmit all messages immediately.

g) I did not think (even dream) from Neal's note he is bitter. I was surprised to get his invitation to visit, and thought it showed great gentility in the writing and the proposal which I accept with rocky belly for sometime in the future. Had I money I would fly out immediately for weekends by plane.

h) Perhaps Neal wants to feel like a crestfallen cuckold because he wants to be beat on the breast with balloons. I well imagine him in that position. Neal's last confession is perhaps yet to be made, tho his salvation is already assured . . . however nobody seems to take seriously the confessions he has made already and continues to do so, which have always had ring of innocency and childlike completeness and have been all he knows, which is more (about himself) than anybody else knows anyway. I believe Neal.

I include his preoccupation and blankness (preoccupation with R.R., household moneying, etc, as final confessions of great merit and value, representing truth to him.

What further sweetness and juiciness issues therefrom no one knows, even him; there is no forcing anything, guilt. (He does not know?) He is already on top of the world. What to do with world is next problem.

Jack probably feels no remorse, just compassion for Neal.

I don't know whether you do or don't want to make Neal feel jealous . . . it's a question for you to answer, but perhaps it is not important to answer it, or it can't be ultimately.

Jack's Mexican plans may or may not go through. Mexico may be a good idea for all of us when we become properly solidified.

Love is not controllable; it can only be offered and accepted . . . you know . . . under the right conditions. As a matter of general course I accept your love and return my own, but it will take a moment of soul-facing and intensity to actually communicate other than words and hopes and general feelings. I don't *know* you like I know Neal, and love is only knowledge. Don't get me wrong. This is no rejection of your desire to come in the middle of the hazy circle, which itself knoweth itself not. Let us arrange all elements to be physically present then.

I am not shipping out I am sure after all.

The moment is ripe for me to be in S.F. South America with Bill and maybe Jack and in N.Y., and I can't be in all three at once. I wish we were all together however. How have we become so scattered?

What we must make plans to do is all meet somewhere where it is practically possible for us to live, under our various pressures, when the practical time comes. Shall we not then keep it in mind to try to arrange for a total grand reunion somewhere for as long as it can last?

I am definitely interested in going to bed with everybody and making love . . . however also I want to say my sexual life has changed a little and with Neal I want him to make love to me. This is something I know, as if the jigsaw puzzle were falling into place. He understands that.

The mileage is too great; we are being tossed around in the cosmic mixing machine. I will make what arrangements I can think of.

Love, Allen

PS Neal: Write me a letter about sex.

A.

Allen's attitude toward sex always managed to raise my Puritan hackles, and I suspect he knew it. It certainly deflated my romantic bubbles. But in other respects his thoughts were reassuring.

Further reassurance was gratefully received from Jack, himself, soon after:

Dear Carolyn:

I was very glad to see that letter you wrote Allen; he sent it for me to see. I had no idea my mail hadn't reached you (one letter to Tennessee and one to Frisco later) and no idea too you and Neal had stopped agreeing on an agree-basis . . . .

I am glad to hear that Neal has a sustained

interest in me, the bastard postures the other way, so naturally, but, ah, um, ahem, ah, . . . Of course he'll rise again . . . and is risen now but as Allen said "Who knows what personal disgust and rocky glare lies beneath Neal's seeming 'silence' . . . after all that's happened, he now has the right to sink into a fit of disgust. — which I wish I could do, it would take the silliness out of me. (I get in on peotl, by the way, disgust, I just ate it twice more times here with the hipsters of Mex. City and Bill, too. I'm not going to take it any more, definitely toxic on the eyes and estamac). Neal is a successful provider because he knows how to work . . . Allen and I never learned tire recapping or braking or any of those difficult or special trades or even tire-changing. I know that Neal will miss (while in Mexico) working . . . and while working in U.S. will miss Mexico . . . if that's what you're going to do. It can be done. I think it would solve problems.

If you and Neal (and I'll probably see you soon) really plan to make it Mexico, then I'll be in on it with you . . . I'll have some sea money and more peace back home. We can all live down here in a house . . . sometimes I'll be either at sea or staying at home in Carolina or visiting Bill in Ecuador . . . Neal sometimes working in California (4 months) and the other 8 writing the First Third in his house in Mexico, with imminent advance . . . sounds logical and awright to me . . . don't want to force anybody . . .

Bill Burroughs says he's going to found his farm on an Ecuadorian high jungle river not far from the coast and invite Hipster Colony of anybody hip come down and found an island in the coming Soviet and Totalitarian invasions of the world.

As for discussing the emotional complexities of the matter, ahem, harrumph, egad, I really feel like Neal — incapable of dealing with such big abstract problems of love and mystery. There is an anxiety in you for Neal to love you in a certain way. What is that certain way? That certain way is lost in a tangle of shrouds if you ask me. I tell you I've always been convinced life is a spook. Many's the time I wanted to hold your hand or kiss you, merely as aknowledgment that we were all in the car heading for the world unknown, but felt jealousy-kick. . . . I don't think Neal was jealous, he just didn't know what we expected him to do, and we didn't either. I personally felt quite calm about the whole thing and still do except for qualms about how you feel, both of you — also, most cruelly, I am at your beck and call to come and go, in other words, I accept loss and death, and if you offer me some of your life I'm very grateful but I know that nothing will come of it, of life, but death, so it really makes no difference to any of us what happens now and soon. . . . Eternity is only thing on my mind permanently, and you are a part of it.

And Oh, incidentally, to conclude this massive epistle, I have already written a third of Dr. Sax in the past month in Mexico . . . in case I catch on like wildfire in New York with On the Road, I got another masterpiece ready for the press. I love you both and hope I don't bore you with my long long talks. Forward my mail. Kiss the grail . . .

He also wrote to Neal, which tidied up the possibiblity of any loose ends in his mind, and all four of us now should know where everybody stood.

Dear Neal,

I know I owe you a bigger letter than this but I'm leaving it up to you to hold on to your reason and know that as ever nothing is changed between us, in other words always were perfect, well-nigh perfect friends. As you said first minute I got to Frisco. "I always like to see a guy do anything he wants" when I was apologizing for feeling like an old fool and saying I hoped I wasn't in the way at suppertime, etc. and you made me realize you WAS my brother, which I've known ever since, and so when circumstances outside you intervened in the balance of that serenity between us I STILL knew it wouldn't affect our closeness and peace — so I'll write just this short note, cause I'm working on Dr. Sax. Now and finally, if you come to Mexico, it will make it greatest place in the world for me — when you are ready to make plans I will be available. I might see you in Frisco next off a ship. No jobs in Mexico as you know.

It surprised me somewhat, although I was delighted as well, that Jack should be outlining a life for us altogether with the men taking turns in residence. I was pleased to think he not only wanted me there, but also that he didn't feel guilty about Neal. On the other hand, I still held out some feelings, hoping Neal would prefer a monogamous arrangement.

Chapter Eleven

Before Allen received Jack's manuscript of *On the Road*, he sent us a hasty note requesting the beginning pages which we still had.

Dear Neal and Caroline:

Received a monumental letter from Jack in Mexico. Jack says you are mad at him or tired of him, Neal, is it true? And also, if you got patience, send me letter summing up general situation for him. I am afraid for him in Mexico; it is a kind of lostness, too, though the things he is doing there are more close to an alone rolling stone — he's smoking with mexicans in mudhuts — I got a sense of absolute freshness or originality in his voyage outwards from world, as if he were really exiled from known world. Can't explain. But write me what happened, in sum, and make sure send me immediately the chapter.

Nothin else now, miss your contact. He says you are busy and obsessed with now complete all-the-way-down-the-line materialistic money and stealing-groceries anxieties, etcetc. also he said he was happy there.

Are you in Frisco, even? What's going on around here?

Love, Allen.

When Allen did receive the completed manuscript of *On the Road* from Jack he exploded:

Why'nt you answer my last letter? too flip? Jack's book arrived and it is a holy mess — it's great all right but he did everything he could to fuck it up

61

with a lot of meaningless bullshit I think page after page of surrealist free association that doesn't make sense to anybody except someone what has blown Jack. I don't think it can be published anywhere in its present state. I know this is an awful hangup for everyone concerned — he must be tired too — but that's how it stands I think. Your tape conversations were good reading; so I could hear what was happening out there — but he put it in entire and seemingly un-unified so it just skips back and forth and touches on things momentarily and refers to events nowhere else in the book; and finally it appears to objective eye so diffuse and disorganized — which it is, on purpose — that it just *don't make.* Jack knows that too, I'll bet. Why is he tempting rejection and fate? Fucking spoiled child, like all of us maybe, but goddam it, it ain't *right* to take on so paranoiac just to challenge and see how far you can go — when there's so much to say and live and do now, how hard it is albeit. Jack is an ignu and I'll bow down to him, but he done fuck up his writing money-wise, and also writing-wise. He was not experimenting and exploring in new deep form; he was purposely just screwing around as if anything he did no matter what he did was O.K., no bones attached. Not purposely, I guess, just drug out and driven to it and in a hole. I don't know what he'll say when I say this to him — he comes back to N.Y. this week or next I think — and how he'll make out with all this shit to shovel around, I dunno. I will try to help but I feel so evil when I not *agree* in blindness. Well shit on this, you get the point.

I still have love longings and yet have not in my lifetime founded a relationship with anyone which is satisfactory and never will unless I change and grow somehow out of this egoistic greyness and squalor. Drifting, like I am or could would leave me with no hope but stolen fruits. Must stop *playing* with my life in a disappointed grey world. Maybe go back to analysis. I am miserable now — not feeling unhappiness, just lack of *life* coming to me and coming out of me — resignation and getting nothing and seeking nothing, staying behind shell — the glare of unknown love, human, unhad by me — the tenderness I never had. I don't want to be just a nothing, a sick blank, withdrawal into myself forever. I can't turn to you for that any more, can't come to Frisco for you because how much you love me, it is still something wrong, not complete, not still enough, not — God knows what not — you know how I was before and what I am, by hangups — do you think that is all I shall get ever, so that is why should I come out? I suppose maybe I'm looking too hung-up at a simple sociable proposition. Well, write me. I would like to hear from you dear Neal.

Allen did tell Jack his opinions, or that's what we assumed, because we got the following mysterious letter from Jack:

Dear Neal & Carolyn:

Just to let you know I'm leaving Mexico City and going to live, write and till my special soils in a small shack type made of dobe bricks in the country not far from here, in a valley . . . for practically and eventually nothing — don't know for how long — will be my headquarters. Won't write for a long time because want to sink into natural oblivion with myself, dog, indian, beautiful and sad indians & — Let my mail dust under a floorboard, see you on some special New Years Eve.

Love and dumb kisses.
My Ma all set at sister's now.

P.S. Eventually I want to go to Ecuador where the mangos, orchids & wives grow wild, no want, no phone hassels, no anger and all that kind of shit ad infinitum. Any important messages for me send to Allen, who will undoubtedly relay them telepathically. Visit me on a burro.

XXX to you and children.   Old Zagg
Write that *First Third* — (love C. sentimentally)

It was like a farewell forever, and Neal and I didn't know what to make of it.

"Oh, he'll come out of it," Neal sighed, "he's just paranoid again and got mad at Allen's rejection. Old Zagg will sit in his mud hut and have himself a regular orgy with Miss Green . . . the bastard, why doesn't he send me some? Awrrgh. Fap." He strode to the window and stood gazing out . . . not at our backyard, I could tell, but at a Mexican valley warmed by a lazy sun where there were no bills, no pressures, just mangos and Miss Green."

Carolyn in 1943, before meeting Neal.

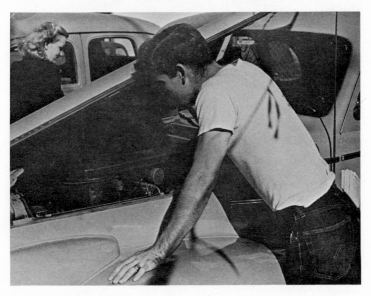

Neal in 1948. (Carolyn in background.)

Jack Kerouac, 1952.

Neal Cassady, 1952.

Neal, Cathy and Jack, 1952.

"Doctor Sax and The Deception of the Sea Shroud"
Comic Strip drawn by Jack Kerouac at kitchen table for Cassady children, 1952 or '53.

Carolyn, Summer 1958.

PART TWO

Fall-Winter 1952-3

Chapter One

Later that year Jack returned to California to live with us. The best times for me were the evenings Jack and I found ourselves alone. We'd both put the children to bed. Jack would read to them in his own unique way; he was so gentle, patient and affectionate. Jamie was his special favorite, and she'd fling her arms around his neck and give him big kisses on the cheek, dissolving him in self-conscious giggles.

Then we'd have our wine and pizza . . . nothing but candlelight . . . romantic music playing in the background. Sometimes we were high and hilarious . . . other times heavily romantic. One such night, when we had finished eating and I'd put the dishes in the sink, we sat sipping our wine, both of us pensive and silent, drinking in the music, the glow of the candle and the vibrant wine. I was drifting peacefully when Jack's voice alerted me, low yet steady, "God . . . I love you."

My heart flipped, my nerves rippled, I was thrown into such turmoil I could manage hardly more than a whisper.

"I can't believe it," I said, and looked up to see his face, his eyes straight on mine, his voice dead serious.

"I could convince you." It was too much . My composure fell apart. My eyes dropped from his to my glass as I desperately fought for a single rational thought. I could only squeeze his hand in return and remain silent, though I knew his eyes had not wavered.

"Let's dance," he said softly.

We floated in a close, timeless embrace; but then my joy was too full to keep up the solemn mood. He filled our glasses, chortling, affecting extravagant chivalrous ges-

73

tures in my adoring eyes, loaded the record player with mambos, and we danced . . . and we danced . . . and we danced . . . abandoned and individual, yet totally immersed in each other and the sensation of being one and together.

For years afterwards, remembering this night, I'd think about Neal. Why couldn't he and I have these romantically emotional love scenes? No one had been more deeply romantic than Neal in the beginning. Did this always cease with the advent of marriage? Did we get so that we knew each other too well? Nevertheless, I never forgot Jack's magic words; they warmed me the rest of my life.

Other memories of those golden months drift by in small but vivid snatches: my sitting on Jack's bed rocking Johnny if he'd wake up crying, Jack propped on one elbow, patting Johnny too, talking to me about his mother, planning when we would meet. He'd read me her letters, and I'd insert comments in his letters to her.

Then there were afternoons when Jack would sit for hours experimenting with the tape recorder, singing both lyrics and "scat," accompanying himself on a tiny pair of bongos I'd given him for a joke. These tapes I listen to now and recall the long fall afternoons, fragrant with the smell of burning leaves, which reminded both of us of our beloved New England, and I relive the quiet pleasure of our being together.

Almost daily he'd go on walks with the girls, listening to their prattle, teaching them to make poems — walks that left their cheeks ruddy, their little fists clenched around precious scraggly flowers he'd helped them pick.

But winter had to come and with it the cold rain and

the colds in the noses. The railroad slowed, and the two men were home more often together, gradually becoming irritated with each other as their private frustrations increased. Neal had to have another car, which brought a day or two of excitement. This one was a Rambler station wagon with better mileage and in better condition than our usual, so that I actually enjoyed driving it — until it, too, turned out to be a lemon and had to be pushed each time it was required to start. I developed a real psychosis about pushing cars before my marriage to Neal was over. A new car made Neal long for driving, and the lure of the big city was increasingly difficult for him to resist, although he couldn't count on Jack's support against me as of old.

Jack, meanwhile, was ever more disgusted with publishers as hassles continued with *On the Road.*

At this time, nothing was going right for him. Jack ranted and growled about the stupidity and cupidity of publishers and their assinine demands, bitterly resenting his failure to be accepted and appreciated. The private rumblings of the two men simmered into a boil and overflowed into our public life. Neal would vent his frustrations in oblique cracks about Jack's presence in the family . . . forgetting completely his own adamant pleas for just that. Jack's supersensitivity and paranoia reacted instantly to an exaggerated degree. There was something about pork chops, I vaguely recall, and Jack's insistence that he'd no longer eat at our table, but would buy himself a hotplate for his room the very next day. I watched them in melancholy disbelief, not knowing how to help. They fought feebly against it; one day they'd be sentimental chums, the next bitter enemies.

In December Jack was laid off by the railroad. In a way he was relieved. He longed again for Mexico, and now nothing prevented his plans. As he thought about it, his tensions slipped from him, replaced by anticipation of the peaceful life he dreamed of. Describing it to me one day he said: "Why don't you come, too, Carolyn? Come and visit me in Mexico, please do."

I was staggered by the unexpected thought. What a fantastic idea. I hardly dared consider it. Jack became more persuasive: "You've never had a vacation . . . not since you married Neal . . . you really should, you know . . . not to go isn't healthy."

I reminded him I had just driven all over the country a year ago. "That can't count," he scoffed. "You've *never* been by yourself, without the children . . . never. Just think of that."

I didn't voice it, but I could have said it never occurred to me that this was a desirable condition once one had accepted the position of wife and mother. I expected — in fact, *chose* to be with my children. But I'd also heard there were advantages to being apart for a time for both parents and children, and though I didn't understand them, I felt I should keep still and consider. It was a temptation. Of course I told Jack, at least, that I loved the idea and would like to, and with that admission he took matters into his own hands and went to Neal. He could not accept the idea without Neal's permission, and, from experience, he had every right to expect Neal to agree.

Without a moment's hesitation Neal endorsed the plan staunchly . . . a bit too much so, it seemed to me. And little by little his attitude changed. Verbally he still insisted he was all for it, but otherwise his behavior became silent, sulky, that of a proper martyr. I could hardly credit my senses. Because of *me?* Neal was feeling rejected by me? And he *cared?* As his resentment became more obvious to both Jack and me, and as his sarcasm toward us increased, we said, "Forget it, Neal, of course we won't do such a thing if you don't like it." And for a few days nothing more was mentioned.

Then, one night when Neal and I were playing pinochle after the children had been put to bed, he said, "Tell you what, I'll make a deal. You let me drive Jack to Mexico now, so's I can get some tea, and I'll agree to let you go when I get back...OK?" Somehow this idea didn't fill me with joy, I felt vaguely that I was being traded for marijuana ... but I couldn't think about it now. Best to stay true to character and talk about practical matters. Casually I played a card.

"Well, how long do you think it would take? Can we afford two trips that long?"

"Yeah, sure, baby. It won't cost a thing. Only the gas. I'll do nothing but drive down, pick up the stuff and drive *right* back ... two days, nothing. The 'grey ghost' is in perfect shape."

Inwardly I had to smile. Practicality had nothing to do with it; he saw another chance to *go.* "Yes, well," I stalled, "I'll think about it."

I thought about it a good deal. Inside, I knew I could never visit Jack, but I'd get angry with myself when I'd realize this. I knew too well I could never leave my children and relax. It didn't fit my idea of motherhood, and it was a pretty serious affront to my marriage vows. Lord knows it was difficult enough for me to uphold any resemblance to my original ideal as it was, but this would be going too far.

I said nothing of my doubts to either man. It would have hurt Jack if I rejected him, and I was intrigued with the idea of Neal as a martyr to me . . . I wondered how serious his pose really was. Meanwhile, no use denying the fact, I enjoyed it. So I thoughtfully agreed to the bargain.

Neal promptly forgot his misery and reverted to his customary cheer when anticipating another "Road" adventure.

The morning of departure arrived. Jack had packed only his sea bag, leaving his manuscripts and books with us to be held until his return East. Neal took very little over and above the essential two pair of socks per day, underwear, toothbrush and a half dozen handkerchiefs. It was a cold, foggy morning, and the children were still asleep. The men stowed their gear in the car and returned to the house singly, taking turns bidding me farewell. Neal was first and played his most dramatic role, kissing me long and intently, hanging on to my hand as he backed away and scanning my face with his tragic love-lorn look. Then he wheeled around and strode across the porch, pausing to look back at the door and utter his standard exit line: "I'll be right back."

I stood beside the kitchen table, trying to keep the appropriate expression on my face as I awaited the second round. Jack held me close a long time, his head buried in my neck. Then he whispered in my ear how we'd be together again in two weeks, not to fail him, he'd get everything ready, Neal would be all right, don't worry. After a brief but tender kiss, he, too, backed slowly out the door, then turned to blow another kiss as he headed down the steps.

Well. I sat down dazed, not knowing whether to laugh or cry, emotions of every kind rising and falling in waves. They were funny, and I couldn't help laughing, although partially from the pleasure of feeling so flattered. I remained in a semi-dream state the rest of the day, going about the household tasks and children's routines only half plugged in.

When I was able to think clearly again I knew at once I'd never go to Mexico, never leave the children, or Neal. But I'd have to wait for Neal's return to find a way out and not lose the ground I'd gained. At least this trip of his left me with no anxieties, no sense of loss, and warmed by the feeling of being loved by two exciting men. I was patient with the children, unharried and serene. What a blessed change for all of us.

Chapter Two

A day or two before Neal's return, I got a letter from him, and although it was no more reassuring than those of other absences, this time there was a ring of truth:

> Dear, dear Wife Carolyn Dolly:
>
> Sitting in the gray ghost Nash in front of Bill Burroughs' house in which Jack and he are sleeping. I write by light of Brakielanternfreightsize.
>
> My heart is bleeding for you. From S.J. to Bakersfield — *first* stop for gas — my thoughts of you filled my mind so that I knew I was composing great love letters. Naturally, I came by lovely things to say to you — mostly it came out — I love *you*.
>
> Stopped in L.A. at dawn at non-existent share-the-ride places, and since it was right on the way, stopped at brother Ralph's and family for 2 slices French toast, then drive down 101 to San Diego — I thought of you — then San Diego to Yuma, Ariz.
>
> Now it is late P.M. daylight and I had not yet given up the wheel. So let Jack drive for 8 miles, then drove because he couldn't — I tell all this later — wait till I get home.
>
> I have got to mail this now. Everything all O.K. Be home Sat. P.M. — leaving here Thurs. A.M. *This is Truth.* I have not and *will not* have touched any kind of any ole female — I am with B.B. and Jack, talking only.
>
> Love, N.

Saturday morning early he spun in the driveway, right on schedule, but he walked in the house like a condemned man, grim and silent. At first I didn't understand. He was tired. He hadn't scored. The car was ruined. What? He talked very little about the trip. Aside from a snide remark or two at Jack's expense, there was nothing to relate; he had just driven, gotten the tea and driven back, What *was* the matter with him?

We were having a cup of coffee at the kitchen table, and he impulsively leaned over and put his head in my lap, squeezing my hand. I stroked his hair and said, "What is it, dear?" but instead of answering me, he got up and walked into the bedroom. I followed him, and there he was, standing in the corner, his forehead against the wall. Ahhh, now I got it . . . but I had to hurry out to stifle my impulse to laugh. So that was it. Now that he'd had his part of our bargain, he was campaigning to get out of keeping the other half — my half.

Maybe this was my out. I'd play his game and pretend he persuaded me not to go. I couldn't spoil a chance to get all this loving attention from him, so it might take awhile, but I certainly couldn't tell him I didn't *want* to go anyway. Not yet.

A letter from Jack sent him into paroxysms of grief again.

Dear Neal & Carolyn:

I took a little dobe block up on Bill's roof, 2 rooms, lots of sun and old Indian women doing the wash. Will stay here awhile even though $12 a month is high rent. But perfect place to write, blast, think, fresh air, sun, moon, stars, the Roof of the City. All ready for your visit, Carolyn, I even bought Mexican pottery to brighten my 2 cells. Tonight I'm buying 3 dozen oysters for 35 cents equivalent (expensive) and frying them in butter, with imported Chianti for a chaser, and French bread. Every morn-

81

ing it's steak and eggs, which I buy for 30 cents and cook up. Also I am stocked on goofballs, bennies, a little laudanum, and Nescafe. Bill finally left Mexico, last night; how sad. They were asking for more bond money. He bequeathed me knives, holsters, daggers, medicines. I feel like Neal that I'll never see him again. Now I'm completely alone on the roof. Now or never with a great new novel long anticipated from me in N.Y. — Day and night tomorrow to it.

Neal, enclosed you'll find note for picking up last half November check. Send it on to me registered mail to my Spanish name, Senor Jean Levesque, or let Carolyn bring it — easier. This is my name now here; the address is too hot to use "Kerouac" — cops come looking for escapee Bill who jumped bond — see?

Carolyn, is you coming? Let me know — write — Love to Cathy, Jamie, Johnny and All.

Love XXX Jack.

Dear Carolyn

Just got your letter. Did Neal get home that night? Thank you for forwarding my mother's letter. I am unbearably lonely in Mexico, I guess I'll never be satisfied with anything. Now that I have regained my regular love of life, of people, specifically of Neal — and you, after October's Darkness, the old human loneliness has come back to wash again my rock, ah me. But what can any of us do with our time? — which runs out while we wait, yawn and worry — Ah phooey. — All the fresh air of the Indian plateau blows into it — Maybe you could drive down with Al Sublette for protection; he wouldn't bother you like Conductors if he knew the purpose of your visit and if Neal said Okay — Mexico, you'll see, has all the practical advantages but the soul yearning broken everywhere. That's

funny about Jamie playing the Jack & Jill record for
me all day long.

I'm trying to rest my feet for railroading next
spring — I've begun my work on the final-chance
big novel.

Come on and get your vacation with me! We'll go
dance the Mambo —

(As usual, Neal did nothing, just like in the
dream I had, he rushed into Mexico City and rushed
out with his tea)

No more paper   XX J.

This almost made me weaken about not going; it
sounded dreamy. If only it weren't so far; if I could just *be*
there. Ah, well. I couldn't watch Neal's agony any more; if
I couldn't go it was best to give up the game and get back
to living. I solemnly told Neal that of course I'd never
leave him if he wanted me. What a relief to see him smile
again, his brow unfurrow, the gloom dispelled.

"Now, how are we going to tell Jack without reactivat-
ing his paranoia?" I got out paper and pen to compose the
"Dear John."

Neal snorted, "Pah, he'll get over it. Serves him right
for stealing other men's wives."

"You keep forgetting, dear heart, it was your idea in
the first place."

"How can you possibly say an untrue thing like that?
Not a bit of it. Why would I do such a stupid thing? Tell
the old boy to get his own girl."

Funny how Jack always seemed to be the cement that
bound our little family together. I sat and mused on the
Christmas now made possible in the big old house. This
year we could have a bigger tree. The mail arrived and in

it a note from Jack. Our problem was solved:

> Dear Carolyn:
>
> Please pardon me for running off to go home for
> Xmas — It looks like I did it on purpose, but it isn't.
> I love you, and I love you for loving me, you —
> What are we gonna do? I'll write, I'm hung up in the
> night — Don't pass up your vacations.
>
> Awful Jack Fool
>
> How is Cathy Doll, Jamie Doll and Johnny Doll?
> and Neal Doll, & you Doll? and me Doll?
> Nobody know.

Poor Jack. He just couldn't be alone. Everything had
worked out for the best, and his mother would be happy,
too.

Chapter Three

We had answered Jack only briefly. Neal procrastinated about sending him his pay over my protestations; I feared this would only cause further strains on our friendship, no matter how positive Neal was that our need was greater. Then I received a long letter from Jack:

Dear Carolyn:

I finally heard from you — thought you were really secretly peeved about Mexico ... and you may be ... But in a way it was better for Neal (I guess)... I really believe . . . your life and vacations is with him. Glad to hear Jamie is "more than ever," I know what you mean, and she'll be ... and is, great. Cathy is a sweet girl; don't underestimate her quiet little soul, honey. I miss my walks around the sidewalks with Cathy and Jamie. I may suddenly come to California for RR, if they recall me, because I may need money . . . but I wouldn't stay at your house again, because the complications are too much, and Neal doesn't appreciate my awareness of everything, and "felt sorry" for me, and I spend less money staying by myself in skid row hotels ... and I don't want to interfere any more with any corner of your hopes and hassels which is really all I've been doing, but only because you asked and the first year Neal asked . . . I told him I wanted to go to Mexico alone, in a bus, and pointed out that as long as he insisted he take me, it was HIS TRIP, not "mine"... blah blahs of eternity ... so, tho I don't want the $30 which is cancellable as unofficial room and board as before the other was, I definitely don't want Neal to chalk the $30 up to the trip to Mexico even in his own secret mind because he remembers what I told him and you weren't there to hear ... poor conniving Neal ... nothing in the world I mind except the

85

possibility that Neal secretly hates me for things he asked me to do and I did because I have always been led around by the nose and never minded neither . . . because I trusted him . . . because when I have something to do finally I do it.

In New York things are very exciting and too much so I want to leave . . . even William Faulkner is here running around having a big time, which he never did before . . . I told Viking Press they'd publish *Doctor Sax* if my name was Faulkner . . . they said they would publish it . . . "at a loss" they predict, if I had another book that would make a gain . . . I do, and am typing it . . . no title, but *great!* (My first Proustian love story).

In old Saybrook I saw a house for sale for $20,000; an aging colonial house still, that faded red-purple of New England, circa 1650. Beautiful stuff and all of its authentic antique and going with a house and 20 ACRES TILLABLE LAND AND ANCIENT OLD HEAVY TREES AND across the field, far, a little cemetery sinking, with faded dates and trees waving in the wind that blows from the sea a mile away . . . if I had money . . . not really . . . Do you want to take a vacation in Mexico still? I'll meet you next week; I'm going for you know what . . . not really . . . . next month. Please sneakily mention to Neal I don't want $30 which is true, but just an ozee by mail. If he does this, I promise in return an ozee of North African Miss Green in cakes . . . which I got free . . . HASHEESH . . . to mix in . . . it's like opium, which is nothing unless mixed with Miss Green . . .

Yes, Carolyn, I'm back on the old beam, but only in moderation and with control, like you always said.

All my best works will be swallowed, imitated, and, like Gertrude Stein, I'll just go to a dumpy grave and who cares . . . LOVE IS ALL THAT COUNTS. I'm glad you love Neal; he certainly loves you, remember that. Adios.

PS: I write you now instead of to Neal . . . is that what you secretly wanted to accomplish? I still suspect that. (Hor, hor hor)

But I loved you one day last Fall so genuinely you'll never know . . . just feel . . . I loved you because you are great, and I'll always love you that way we loved, till graves soon sinking fields. . . .

Poor, dear Jack. I couldn't deny the pleasure I felt at the declaration of his love. I had already pretty well decided married life with Jack on a daily basis would never work. He was far too moody, his feelings too touchy, too wrapped up in himself. This "self" consciousness might be just the thing that made him a good writer. He could observe and report with brilliant clarity all the teeming life a-round him, but his efforts to partake of it and lose himself in it were generally disappointing; he felt threatened and alone . . . and he retreated. Perhaps that was one of the fascinations Neal held for him. He envied Neal's ability to make life happen; to be a principal in the action, not a bystander. And his love-making too. He had an air of apology. I didn't feel that he ever gave or received completely. All our good times were due mainly to my staying constantly alert to his moods and desires. I was allowed to share his observations, which I enjoyed, and he liked company, as long as it was sympathetic. I knew better than to disagree or question his inner motives, an area where he could never be objecive.

I'd never known a man with such a tender heart, so much sweetness. Could this be the reason for his withdrawal? Was he ashamed to be gentle and compassion-ate? Sometimes he put on a show of bravado and coarse-ness, and it never failed to embarrass me, it was so

obviously phony. Like *On the Road*: that wasn't Jack, just
an imitation based on Neal's behavior. I remembered in
the beginning when I first met him how he used to brag
about getting into fist fights if some guy cast aspersions
on his toughness. Big football hero, humph. But I had to
admit that was the type society presented as the criterion
of a "real" man. Of course he had to be drunk to act that
way, which was probably why he was never far from a
bottle of wine.

Chapter Four

Neal left shortly thereafter for two weeks on a railroad hold down. When his return was delayed, he sent me a huge bunch of red roses. Instead of cheering me up, it only made me long for him all the more. He had never ever sent me flowers before, and I felt like crying all day. Knowing how I felt, his letters tried to soothe:

Who's your ever lovin' daddy? Didn't he spend his last $5 foolishly to send red roses to his own sweet blue lady? Will you be my Valentine every day?

Today I'm the loneliest yet; I mean lonely, alone and cut off from all but you, and it scares me; I realize how much I need you and how hopeless I am without you ... and even with you. Will you hold my sad head and soothe the savage beast? Pathos and passion that twirl toward my heart each time I think of you, who is all there is, all five feet two, between me and the gallows death I dread ... or am I morbidly insane to jumble up all the tender things you are and squash them into my tiny mind to bubble and hold me down from exploding.

Songs mean so much to me. Will you sing to me in our bedroom that we depapered and painted? Love songs?

His efforts succeeded: I stiffened my lip and wrote:

Feel fine this AM, all rarin to go again. (I know it all depends on Cathy ... so far all well ... hope every day to keep it) Love you SO! We have great plans, but all depends on daddy. Who knows, if you love me all sorts of miracles may happen. Is it really

89

possible? I've never known any real, close, lasting love, you know. Perhaps not being really close to my parents has made it hard for me to be close to Cathy or you. I've only experienced the illicit temporary and "safe" (insofar as permanent responsibility and demands). The real thing is a constant test and a tough one. I want so much to make it a natural and desirable process. Can you save us all? Do you want to? I can't believe I can be worth it to you. Tell me what you want me to do and how you want me to be and what sort of picture you have of the woman you love so I can try living up to it. You're altogether too uncritical.

And thus I hung on another two weeks, at the end of which:

Dear Baby:

It's gone from bad to worse: hold onto yourself... THEY WON'T RELEASE ME! But they *must* before March 13, cause that's when I have to be back on the Coast Division. So lookie here, it's really for the best . . .

And he desperately tried to convince me by outlining our need for the money, detailing his own loneliness, praising my help and planning all the household and garden tasks he was eager to engage in, "I'm only sorry I'm not handy . . . and could make toys for the kids," and three or four pages of love. But my house of fortitude was built on sand, and it tumbled down around him.

90

Dear Neal:

Good thing that was such a sweet letter. This has been a blue weekend and a worse morning. I got up feeling like someting had been put over on me again, but I'm fighting the impulse to believe it. Last night I got panicky and felt I just couldn't stand it another minute. Five years of the waiting, the last days of expecting you being the hardest . . . I go around keeping everything straightened, brushing my hair, dressing me and the kids to look pretty for daddy and hearing every car all night within miles, even though I try not to listen. All for nothing . . . again and again. And now that everything is supposed to be right, and we're just about to *begin* . . . why can't we begin? Why can't we have it now?

The washing machine busted, and Johnny has a fever this AM. So I guess the money you're making is what I should be blessing, and you for perserving instead of whining and complaining. That damn RR rules everything. I'm tired of playing second fiddle to that too. Now that you say you want me, where are you? I wasn't going to write at all to avoid saying all these things, but now that I've blabbed it all out, I can at least say I know you aren't to blame and are torn between all the demands I make on you and trying to do your best . . . it is THE best. I think you're terrific. Don't worry, I'll make it and not take it out on you any more.

Jack wrote a note asking you to write him a word about RR. He seems to be afraid the men don't like him, and he'll have a bad time or somethin. I don't get it. Such an affliction he has . . . what does he care what they think? Far as I can tell nobody thinks much about anybody.

The hoghead said he'd build the fence and remove the old shack since Marie and I cut the vines. Everybody jumps when the Cassadys move in, wot? I love you. I'm afraid to think of it. B. Goodman on radio playing "My Guy's Come Back". . . thought I'd

91

be singing that too.

In spite of my resolve, my self-pity persisted:

> Sunday is too awful... our peaceful living room...
> all rearranged, is fine for funnies and the concert
> and the almond tree almost thru blooming. I'm sick
> of telling you of things I enjoyed you are never here
> to share. We've had so *little* time "together." I fear
> again you've found other interests, and that's no
> good an attitude.
> A big drunk just walked right in the front door.
> I'm still shaking. He said he wanted food. I gave
> him 50¢ cause I couldn't get him out. He grabbed
> Johnny and kissed him. Johnny screamed. The guy
> cried... (he has 3 of his own) I called the landlord
> for a lock. Think of all the times, especially nite I go
> to Forest's for hours. Wish I had a husband at such
> times... damn the money... if it means this. I guess
> I'm incorrigibly selfish. Do as you think best. I hope
> the call back will let you compromise. I'll *try* not to
> be bitter again . . .
>
> Love. C.

Undaunted by my whining, Neal continued his cheer
and encouragement. Although he gave me a factual ac-
count of his deadly hot days and cold lonely nights, he
never complained. How did he manage it? I told him he
should; it was part of my job to comfort him as well. But
no, in fact, I never ever remember him complaining
about anything that had to do with us. Even my selfish
letters he'd answer with extravagant praise, seeing only
good.

92

Dear Carolyn,

When I get home we'll be in our rearranged bedroom and read again to each other all our love letters . . . all too few they are, so we'll make up for it by telling each other, mouth to ear, all the things we feel and all we want to say and have wanted to say forever. Just remember this: I have solved our sex problem. Don't forget to remind me to tell you about it when I get home.

Love, Neal.

A special limited edition of one hundred fifty copies, bound in boards by Cardoza-James, has been numbered and signed by the author.